100 + Fun Ideas

D1461051

Transition Times

Eileen Jones

Other Titles in the 100+ Fun Ideas Series:

Practising Modern Foreign Languages
in the Primary Classroom....................... 978-1-903853-98-6
Art Activities... 978-1-905780-33-4
Playground Games 978-1-905780-40-2
Science Investigations.............................. 978-1-905780-35-8
Wet Playtimes 978-1-905780-32-7

Published by Brilliant Publications
Unit 10, Sparrow Hall Farm
Edlesborough, Dunstable
Bedfordshire, LU6 2ES, UK
www.brilliantpublications.co.uk

Sales and stock enquiries:
Tel: 01202 712910
Fax: 0845 1309300
E-mail: brilliant@bebc.co.uk
General information enquiries:
Tel: 01525 222292

The name Brilliant Publications and the
logo are registered trademarks.

Written by Eileen Jones
Illustrated by Emily Skinner

© Text Eileen Jones 2009
© Design Brilliant Publications 2009

ISBN 978-1-905780-34-1
First printed and published in the UK in
2009

The right of Eileen Jones to be identified
as the author of this work has been
asserted by herself in accordance with
the Copyright, Designs and Patents Act
1988.

Contents

Preface   7

Activity		Key Stage		Subject grouping	Page

Chapter 1   Morning arrival   8–26

	Activity	Key Stage		Subject grouping	Page
1.	Monday morning smiles	KS1	KS2	Art and design	9
2.	Hotel guests	KS1	KS2	Literacy	9
3.	What a rush!	KS1	KS2	Numeracy	10
4.	Book critics		KS2	Literacy	11
5.	On TV!		KS2	Literacy	12
6.	Hit the target		KS2	Numeracy	13
7.	Strange sayings	KS1	KS2	Literacy	14
8.	In the news		KS2	Geography; Literacy	14
9.	Bulls Eye!		KS2	Numeracy	15
10.	Help wanted!	KS1	KS2		16
11.	Postboxes	KS1	KS2	Literacy	17
12.	Passports, please	KS1	KS2	Literacy	17
13.	Morning Sudoku		KS2	Numeracy	18
14.	Ladder scramble		KS2	Literacy	19
15.	Clues to the past		KS2	History	19
16.	In the post		KS2	Literacy	20
17.	Teacher in trouble!	KS1	KS2	Numeracy	21
18.	Shopping trolleys		KS2	Numeracy	21
19.	Tricky trolleys		KS2	Numeracy	22
20.	Memorable mnemonics		KS2	Literacy	22
21.	X marks the spot		KS2	Geography	23
22.	Landmarks	KS1	KS2	Geography	24
23.	Weather watchers	KS1	KS2	Geography	24
24.	Breakfast buns	KS1	KS2	Numeracy	25
25.	Today's words are		KS2	Literacy	26
26.	Spellcheck	KS1	KS2	Literacy	26

Chapter 2   Register time   27–31

	Activity	Key Stage		Subject grouping	Page
27.	Talking food	KS1	KS2	Science	28
28.	Talking leisure	KS1	KS2		28
29.	Funny names		KS2	Literacy	29
30.	Active answers	KS1	KS2	Literacy	29
31.	Hello, hello, hello		KS2	MFL	30
32.	In role	KS1	KS2		31

Activity	Key Stage		Subject grouping	Page

Chapter 3   All in a line   32–38

Activity	KS1	KS2	Subject	Page
33. Filing children	KS1	KS2	Literacy	33
34. After you		KS2	Literacy; Numeracy	34
35. Is that my name?		KS2	Literacy	34
36. Wakey! Wakey!	KS1	KS2		35
37. At the bus stop	KS1	KS2	PE	36
38. Mini-workout	KS1	KS2	PE	37
39. Walking dictionaries		KS2	Literacy	38

Chapter 4   Changing location   39–49

Activity	KS1	KS2	Subject	Page
40. Walking filing cabinets	KS1	KS2		40
41. Target points	KS1	KS2		41
42. Walk like … mice	KS1	KS2		42
43. Cross the bridge	KS1	KS2		42
44. Instant growing	KS1	KS2	PE	43
45. D for deportment		KS2	History; PE	44
46. Football fit!		KS2	PE	44
47. Where am I?	KS1	KS2	Geography	45
48. Alliterative answers		KS2	Literacy	46
49. Humming bees	KS1	KS2	Music	46
50. Happy as we go!	KS1	KS2	Music; Literacy	47
51. Observation!		KS2		47
52. Quizmaster		KS2		48
53. Look out!	KS1	KS2		48
54. Whisper, whisper	KS1	KS2		49

Chapter 5   Starting the afternoon   50–66

Activity	KS1	KS2	Subject	Page
55. Time for everything	KS1	KS2	Numeracy	51
56. Eat well!	KS1	KS2	Science	52
57. Balanced eaters	KS1	KS2	Science	52
58. Dear Ed …	KS1	KS2		53
59. Let's go to …	KS1	KS2	Geography	54
60. Afternoon blog		KS2	Literacy	55
61. Fishy folk	KS1	KS2	Art and design	55
62. Clever clues		KS2	History	56
63. Picture the food	KS1	KS2		56
64. Musical inspirations	KS1	KS2	Music	57
65. What will I say?		KS2	Literacy	58
66. Picture the story		KS2	Literacy	59
67. Add the words		KS2	Literacy	60

Activity			Key Stage	Subject grouping	Page

Chapter 5 Starting the afternoon (cont.) 50–66

	Activity	Key Stage		Subject grouping	Page
68.	Marching songs	KS1	KS2	Literacy; Music	61
69.	Lost for words!		KS2	Literacy	62
70.	Still waiting for that bus!	KS1	KS2	PE	63
71.	That's a funny story!		KS2	Literacy	64
72.	What's my cue?		KS2	Literacy	65
73.	Stress-buster	KS1	KS2	Art and design	65
74.	How does it work?	KS1	KS2	Art and design	66

Chapter 6 Circle time 67–87

	Activity	Key Stage		Subject grouping	Page
75.	The magic talk box	KS1	KS2	Literacy	68
76.	I never knew that!	KS1	KS2	Literacy	69
77.	Discovery of the week	KS1	KS2	Literacy	69
78.	Spot the Chief	KS1	KS2		70
79.	Follow that story …		KS2	Literacy	71
80.	We have a problem!		KS2		72
81.	Find the solution!		KS2		72
82.	Classroom code (Part 1)		KS2		73
83.	Classroom code (Part 2)		KS2		73
84.	Pass the question parcel		KS2		74
85.	Catch this mood!	KS1	KS2		75
86.	All at sea	KS1	KS2	Art and design	76
87.	Parachute fun	KS1	KS2	PE; Geography	77
88.	Shipwreck survivors		KS2		78
89.	Pipedreams	KS1	KS2		79
90.	Making improvements		KS2	Literacy	80
91.	Toss the rhyme	KS1	KS2	Literacy	81
92.	Soothometer	KS1	KS2		82
93.	A is for …		KS2	Literacy	83
94.	Pond challenge	KS1	KS2		84
95.	Hear the signs	KS1	KS2		85
96.	All in a ring	KS1			86
97.	Ed says …	KS1	KS2		87
98.	Well done!	KS1	KS2		87

Chapter 7 Changing lesson 88–97

	Activity	Key Stage		Subject grouping	Page
99.	Recharge the brain battery	KS1	KS2		89
100.	Guesstimate	KS1	KS2	Numeracy	90
101.	Follow on		KS2	Numeracy	91
102.	Word associations	KS1	KS2		91
103.	Pleased to meet you	KS1	KS2		92

Activity	Key Stage		Subject grouping	Page

Chapter 7   Changing lesson (cont.)   50–66

104. Switch off! Switch on!	KS1	KS2		93
105. On the catwalk	KS1	KS2	PE	94
106. Square dancing		KS2	PE	95
107. Take five!	KS1	KS2	PE	96
108. Opposites		KS2	Literacy	97

Chapter 8   The end of the day   98–122

109. Target totals	KS1	KS2	Numeracy	99
110. Interactive story fun	KS1	KS2		100
111. Hotel satisfaction	KS1	KS2	Numeracy	101
112. Clocking off	KS1	KS2		102
113. The big conversation		KS2	Science; Literacy	102
114. Time management		KS2	Numeracy	103
115. School landmarks		KS2	Geography	104
116. Who's that on the carpet?	KS1	KS2		105
117. Test the teacher	KS1	KS2		106
118. Awards ceremony	KS1	KS2		107
119. See you again!	KS1	KS2		108
120. Who am I?		KS2		109
121. Changing teachers	KS1	KS2		110
122. Time for tea!	KS1	KS2	Numeracy	111
123. Fly the flag		KS2	Geography	112
124. The 'hello' game		KS2	MFL	113
125. Time to say goodbye		KS2	MFL	114
126. Let's sing	KS1	KS2		115
127. Storyland characters	KS1	KS2		116
128. Music time	KS1	KS2		117
129. How was your day?	KS1	KS2		118
130. Time to relax	KS1	KS2		119
131. I-spy with a difference!	KS1	KS2		120
132. It's storytime (Part 1)		KS2	Literacy	121
133. It's storytime (Part 2)		KS2	Literacy	122

Preface

This book is crammed with stimulating ideas for the awkward, transition times of the day. Although short occasions, these can be the times that present teachers with the most difficulties. The activities here are chosen carefully, with the occasions and the children's likely needs in mind. Nevertheless, you are the expert on your own class. You know what will most benefit them now: a game, relaxation, exercise, or talking to and getting to know one another. Therefore, select what you want when you want it, choosing the activity to fit that day's timetable, weather, or stage of the year.

Many of the day's transition times vary in length from day to day (your end of the day session may be longer sometimes than others) or from child to child (not everyone arrives at school at the same time). You can avoid frustrating, unfinished activities by tying up loose ends in a later lesson in the day or with homework. Alternatively, many of the activities have links to ideas in other chapters of the book, so avoiding the children feeling they are time-filling.

The aim of these ideas is to make the classroom a happy place to return to. Therefore, the activities are both enjoyable and hold the children's interest. In addition, they foster important attitudes:

- ✧ Involvement with classmates
- ✧ Working as a team
- ✧ Physical and mental health
- ✧ Self-esteem

Resources recommended are trouble-free. Nevertheless, be smart: if you make a resource, save it as hardcopy or a file for your interactive whiteboard (IWB). That way, activities can be repeated, while simple adaptations of a resource are often suggested for a second activity.

Finally, remember to have fun! These activities are meant to be enjoyed. They will refresh repetitive routines, such as lining-up and answering the register, and they will smoothly link the changes of focus or environment. It is because of these that the rest of the day will go well.

With these activities in place, the rest of the day will run smoothly.

Chapter 1
Morning arrival

Morning arrival can set the pattern of the whole day. For the best start, your classroom needs to be welcoming, friendly and inclusive. Children are happiest with an immediate focus and these activities offer them something to do, look at or talk about. They are purposeful, yet fun.

Not everyone may arrive at the same time, but you can avoid the need for repeated explanations by giving advance details of an activity on a previous day, or encouraging children to inform later arrivals of what they are doing. Help yourself further by preparing instructions or resources in advance, so they are ready for speedy display. Time spent preparing and saving computer files for an IWB is particularly worthwhile: it becomes easy to repeat ideas such as *Teacher in trouble* (Activity 17) or to create a new activity from *Shopping trolleys* (Activity 18).

These staggered arrival times often make it impossible to ensure that everyone completes an activity. Many of these suggestions deliberately lend themselves to being followed up in one of that day's lessons, an end-of-day game or discussion, or a homework task.

You know best the mood you want to establish, so select a week's activities to respond to your class's current needs. For example, *Passports, please* (Activity 12) is an excellent way to learn more about everyone at the start of the year; *Help wanted!* (Activity 10) makes everyone feel needed; and *Breakfast buns* (Activity 24) is a calm, absorbing activity for a lively class.

1. Monday morning smiles   KS1, KS2

✦   Put a piece of card at everyone's place.

✦   Write this challenge on the whiteboard:

Make a happy face to banish Monday morning blues.

✦   Ask the children to create cardboard faces – perhaps of clowns.

✦   Try them out later to see which one puts the quickest smile on the most faces.

✦   Use them to make an instant happiness display, or as inspiration for poetry or story writing.

2. Hotel guests   KS1, KS2

✦   Create a form, with space for a child's name and two large and one small writing sections. Photocopy it and put one at everyone's place.

✦   Make your classroom a hotel! You, as hotel doorman, meet and greet guests on arrival.

✦   Wearing your uniform jacket or hat, welcome children by name, trying to have a personal comment for everyone.

✦   In role, direct children to their rooms (their tables) to fill in the first section of the form with their achievement hopes for today. (For younger children, simplify this to what they hope to most enjoy or do well at. Representation could be pictorial.)

✦   Make sure that forms are retained for the afternoon, with the bottom section empty *Hotel satisfaction* (Activity 111).

3. **What a rush!** KS1, KS2

✦ Ask the children to consider how they would answer this question: Has it seemed a rush to get here on time?

✦ Suggest they discuss the question with a partner or small group.

✦ They will need to write down data: when they got up; how long it is since then; what they have done in that time; how long they have spent on different tasks. (For younger children, concentrate on pictorial representation in chronological sequence.)

✦ Ask them to keep the data for this afternoon *Time management* (Activity 114).

4. **Book critics**

✦ Tell the children that they are going to become book reviewers.

✦ Choose about six (illustrated) books, of varying levels, one per group or table.

✦ Ideally, each table should have multiple copies of their book, to make reading easier.

✦ Tell the children to read the opening pages.

✦ The children must become book reviewers, asking themselves: Does the book seem promising? Would I choose it? For which year group?

✦ Let them make individual notes before comparing views with others on their table. Can they reach group decisions?

✦ Follow this up in a literacy lesson, the children listening to one another's discussions and verdicts.

5. **On TV!** KS2

✦ On the whiteboard, write 5–7 letters that can make a number of words.

✦ Use the format of the television programme 'Countdown': words (one to seven letters long) have to be made from the letters.

✦ List rules – misspellings will not count as words.

✦ Extend the game with scoring: the longer the word, the greater its value. As children improve, use letters that are an anagram of a seven-letter word; solving it carries bonus points!

✦ You could compare results in the word part of your literacy lesson.

F D R E U A M

6. **Hit the target**

✦ Set and write up a class target for the week – for example, 35 house points.

✦ Announce this week's target reward – perhaps a bonus Friday afternoon instalment of a TV serial.

✦ Display a list of points' allocation, for example:
  ✧ a working level of noise during a lesson – 2 points
  ✧ no coats on the cloakroom floor – 2 points

✦ Use a corner of the whiteboard to jot down points during the day.

✦ Make and display a days of the week chart, so you can keep a daily running total.

	Monday	Tuesday	Wednesday	Thursday	Friday	
Tidy cloakroom						
Clear desks						
Science Corner						
TOTAL						

7. **Strange sayings** KS1, KS2

✦ Put a postcard-size piece of paper at each place.

✦ Write a selection of common idioms on the whiteboard, for example: Raining cats and dogs.

✦ Ask the children to produce a vivid illustration of one of the idioms.

✦ If time, ask them to use the idiom in conversation with a partner. Can they write a more ordinary way to say the same thing?

✦ At literacy time, compare results. Make a display, matching idioms, pictures and readily-understood words.

8. **In the news** KS2

✦ Having encouraged the children to view themselves as newspaper reporters, give out paper for them to submit their latest article.

✦ Make your focus appropriate to the age group. You could link it to current geography work. Reports could include comments about school activities, happenings in the area, changes to the local environment or national news.

✦ Use the articles for display on a News board.

✦ Collaborate to publish group newspapers; or appoint an editorial team to select articles for a weekly class newspaper.

9. **Bull's eye!** KS2

✦ Write six numbers between 1 and 100 on the whiteboard. In a different colour write a target answer – for example, 207. This number is the bull's eye.

✦ Using any or all of the six numbers (one time each) and any of the four operations (+, -, x, ÷) the children must reach an answer as close as possible to the bull's eye. They need to record their working.

✦ Let the children set a bull's eye puzzle for a partner.

✦ In the numeracy lesson starter, compare results. How close are answers to the target? Which numbers were used? Did anyone hit the target bull's eye.

✦ As the children improve, look for target numbers that can be hit exactly, sometimes by strange and assorted methods.

1   5   13 20   70 85

Using +, −, x and ÷

Calculate as near as possible to 207

Don't forget to show workings out.

10. **Help wanted!** KS1, KS2

✦ Think of 10–12 classroom jobs you are likely to do at the start of the day (switching on computers; loading programs; tidying the bookcase; giving out marked books; re-filling pen and pencil pots).

✦ Confess that you feel overworked! Would the children be willing to help?

✦ Create enthusiasm by emphasizing the children's role will be voluntary, but greatly appreciated. Write a job description for each volunteer task on card. Photocopy and laminate the cards.

✦ Put a card at each place, offering the same task to two or three children.

✦ Vary your job grouping in order to encourage new relationships among the children and to make everyone feel equally important.

11. **Postboxes** KS1, KS2

✦ Draw four postboxes on the whiteboard.

✦ Label each with a word beginning, making your choices relevant to your current spelling work, for example tri, bi, sub and tele for older children.

✦ Ask the children to think of about eight words for each box.

✦ Emphasize that correct spelling is more important than a large number of words, so encourage the use of dictionaries for checking.

12. **Passports, please** KS1, KS2

✦ Make a passport form for the children to complete.

✦ Provide spaces for a picture, appearance description, personal details, hobbies, friendships and special information.

✦ Use the completed passports to create a friendly, inclusive display.

✦ Occasionally, in order to update passports, ask the children to complete a fresh form.

✦ The updated information may alert you to a need to change your class seating plan or your grouping for volunteer tasks, as you realise that someone is feeling excluded from the friendship groups.

13. Morning Sudoku KS2

✦ In a previous numeracy session, introduce Sudoku puzzles. (Most daily newspapers carry examples.)

✦ Photocopy a puzzle for the children to complete. (Make it more manageable by completing plenty of squares.)

✦ Display it on the IWB, and demonstrate working out a square's number.

✦ Increase confidence by pencil use (it can be erased) and partner collaboration.

✦ In the numeracy lesson go through the result, or let children finish the puzzle for homework.

14. Ladder scramble KS2

✦ Write some pairs of words on the whiteboard, one of the pair at the top of the board, one below it at the bottom.

✦ Explain that you want the bottom word to change into the top word by climbing as short a ladder as possible. List the rules:
   ✧ only one letter may be changed at a time;
   ✧ the letter change must create a real word;
   ✧ each change counts as a new rung of the ladder.

✦ Work out an example on the whiteboard. Then give the children easy ones to begin with so that they gain confidence.

✦ Use the results for spelling revision in literacy time.

✦ Compare the ladders made. Which pair of words produced the shortest ladders?

15. Clues to the past KS2

✦ Ask the children to think about this year's history topics. They must choose a figure from the past, but one whose name the rest of the class should know from their history work.

✦ The children are going to become that person. At a masked ball, with their identity concealed, what clever clues could they give about who they are?

✦ Ask the children to make up and write no more than ten clues to their person. The clues must not be too easy!

✦ Save the clues for when you come back in the afternoon (see *Clever clues*, Activity 62).

16. In the post

✦ Use the computer to create a page of small rectangles. Suggest these are letters that are in your postbag. Unfortunately, the names typed on them are very similar: they all use the letter string –ough. You need them sorted by pronunciation.

✦ Save the file, ideally for later use on the IWB, print and copy for everyone.

✦ Draw a number of postboxes on the whiteboard. If needed, give each a 'sounds like ... ' label, for example: sounds like 'off'; sounds like 'uff'.

✦ Ask the children to sort the mail. If the children work with a partner, saying words to each other, they will find it helpful.

✦ Make the activity appropriate to the children's current spelling level, adapting it for younger children by asking them to sort into sets of words with the same vowel phonemes or digraphs.

17. Teacher in trouble   KS1, KS2

✦   Use your whiteboard as a notice board, onto which the Head has pinned tasks you must do this evening!

✦   At the side of the whiteboard, write the number of hours you have available this evening. How will you fit all the jobs in?

✦   Set the children the problem-solving task of producing a timetable for you.

✦   In numeracy, share some of the timetables to see if they work. Will you have any minutes to spare?

✦   For younger children, simplify the task to pictorial representation in chronological sequence.

18. Shopping trolleys   KS2

✦   Turn your whiteboard into a shop window, with today's bargains and prices on display. Creating this shop window on the IWB as it will allow you to save and re-use it another day.

✦   At the side of the board, draw your transparent purse, the coins clearly visible.

✦   Ask the children to use the money in the purse to do your shopping, perhaps for the ingredients of a balanced evening meal or a healthy lunch.

✦   The children should draw a shopping trolley with their choices and the shop's till receipt showing the total.

✦   How much is left in the purse?

19. Tricky trolleys   KS2

✦ Return to previous lesson (Activity 18).

✦ You could now vary the problem-solving task, prices, or money in your purse.

✦ Set new challenges by:
   ✧ asking the children to produce alternative trolleys for you to choose from;
   ✧ setting a spending limit that still leaves £1 or more in your purse;
   ✧ demanding the largest number of items possible with the money in your purse.

✦ Which trolley do you think is best value for your money?

20. Memorable mnemonics   KS2

✦ Ask the children – perhaps with a partner – to look at their current homework spelling list.

✦ Is there a word they, or classmates, are likely to have problems with? For example, surprise.

✦ Ask the children to compose a memorable mnemonic to help everyone remember the correct spelling.

✦ Share some of the results in the word section of your literacy lesson.

✦ Use favourites for display on a spelling board, adding to them regularly.

21. **X marks the spot** KS2

✦ Draw, or create with a computer, a map of a desert island. Include plenty of features: for example, a large rock, a twisted tree, a tall palm.

✦ Mark compass points at the top of the map.

✦ Make a copy for every child, retaining your original map.

✦ The children (pirates) are burying their treasure on the island. They must choose their spot and mark it with an X.

✦ They need to write accurate clues in order to find the spot again. Use the clues during geography to revise direction and compass points. A pirate can read out clues as the others study your unmarked map on the IWB. Can anyone locate the missing treasure?

✦ Vary this activity by creating different environments.

22. Landmarks KS1, KS2

✦ Ask the children to think about their journey to school. What is the most memorable landmark? Ask the children to draw a picture of it.

✦ Stress the need for other people to be able to recognize it and its location. Do they need to add a sketch map?

✦ Ask them to make notes about the landmark and why it is particularly important to them and their journey.

✦ Find a speaking and listening opportunity when the children present and talk about their landmark pictures to the class. Consider using your scanner to let the children show them on the IWB.

23. Weather watchers KS1, KS2

✦ Put this question on the whiteboard: What is the weather like this morning?

✦ Provide paper for an up-to-date picture. Depending on age, the children may be able to add the time, temperature, the correct weather symbol or a Beaufort scale symbol.

✦ Suggest they pretend to be the TV weather presenter. Ask them to write what they would say if they had a one minute weather slot on the radio; perhaps they could include special advice for drivers or warnings of icy pavements for pedestrians.

✦ Set aside a classroom Weather Watching notice board for these reports. Consider updating the board in the afternoon.

24. **Breakfast buns** KS1, KS2

✦ Make a durable resource for this activity by cutting out and laminating magazine pictures.

✦ Hang the 'Café open' sign above your whiteboard.

✦ Display today's ingredients, for example: sausage, bacon, tomato, mushrooms, lettuce. Add or reduce the number of ingredients as appropriate to age and ability.

✦ Set the challenge:
   ✧ everything is sold in a bun;
   ✧ buns always contain three items;
   ✧ how many different sorts of buns can the children draw or list for today's menu?

25. Today's words are ...   KS2

✦   Write five to ten words on the whiteboard; make them relevant to curriculum work to be done later in the day (for example, science, geography, history).

✦   Give out dictionaries. Ask the children to look up the meanings of the words. Then they should write their own definitions in clear, brief language.

✦   Can the children sort the words into an alphabetical glossary?

✦   When you begin the relevant lesson later in the day, agree on and display a class reference glossary of the words.

26. Spell check   KS1, KS2

✦   Write these words in a vertical list on the whiteboard: Look, Say, Cover, Write.

✦   Emphasize the correct sequence of the actions. Suggest that doing this will make them as reliable as a computer Spell check!

✦   Do the children think they are progressing well with leaning their spellings for this week?

✦   Suggest they find out, concentrating on one word at a time, and going through the sequence of actions two or even three times.

✦   Encourage them to identify the ones that keep giving them problems. Can a partner suggest a clever way to remember the correct spelling?

✦   Are they close to being as reliable as the computer Spell check?.

Chapter 2
Register time

Register time may be short, but it has great importance. You need an accurate attendance record for official figures and possible emergency situations, such as a fire alarm. Consequently, from the start of the year, establish this as a period when all the class concentrate on what is said and heard.

In addition to viewing register time as an opportunity to improve speaking and listening skills, view it also as an opportunity for fun. The routine of ordinary methods of the register can become mundane, so intersperse your usual format with some of these ideas. The fact that the children then have to think about something other than their name avoids them becoming bored, chatty and inattentive.

27. Talking food KS1, KS2

✦ Tell the children your personal target for this week: to eat well.

✦ Each morning, when you call the register, you want the children to make a food reply.

✦ Afterwards you will choose ingredients for your meal(s) from their replies.

✦ Use your choices to reinforce science learning on healthy eating and a balanced diet.

✦ Bring the activity to life by sometimes producing the chosen food(s) in your next day's packed lunch.

28. Talking leisure KS1, KS2

✦ Announce a new personal target this week: to make better use of your after-school or pre-school free time.

✦ Suggest that this could involve an after-school hobby or pre-school exercise.

✦ Ask the children to answer the register with a suggestion. Afterwards choose one that you agree to try for one day of the week.

✦ By the end of the week, your selections could stress a healthy balance between physical and mental exercise, individual and shared activity.

✦ Enlist the children's help in drawing up your timetable.

29. Funny names KS2

✦ Suggest that the children answer the register with alliterative adjective before their name.

✦ Give them an example about yourself: talkative teacher.

✦ Use the same format for a few days, so children can begin to have ideas ready.

✦ At the end of the register, award a team point, house point or stick-on smile to the person whose name was most memorable.

✦ Keep the enjoyment factor, by emphasizing that a straightforward name is always correct. The added adjective is a bonus!

✦ Combine this with *Alliterative answers* (Activity 48).

30. Active answers KS1, KS2

✦ Use a similar format to *Funny names* (previous activity) but this time the children answer with a verb and their name.

✦ Encourage the children to use action verbs and to demonstrate them.

✦ Give them an example about yourself: tapping teacher.

✦ Accompany the phrase with an appropriate action (tap your fingers on the table).

✦ At the end of the register, select the one you thought most original. Make your reward a request for a special repeat performance.

31. Hello, hello, hello KS2

✦ Link this idea to *The 'hello' game* (Activity 124).

✦ Once the children have become familiar with how to say Hello in different languages, give them regular practice at register time.

✦ Choose a country and put the flag on display so the children know where they are.

✦ When you call the children's names, they should answer with Hello in the appropriate language.

✦ Extend the activity, so that the children may say Hello in any language they choose.

✦ Perhaps they will surprise you one morning with a new language. You could add that country's flag and greeting to *Fly the Flag* activities (Activity 123).

"Hola"   "Hello"

"Guten Tag"

"Bonjour"

"Ciao"

32. In role KS1, KS2

✦ Link this to *Help wanted!* (Activity 10).

✦ Suggest the children answer the register in role. They will need to think of a short, snappy job-title.

✦ For example, if your name was called, you might reply with 'Register marker' here.

✦ This game will give the children good practice in using nouns. If they get stuck, your job description cards from Activity 10 should help.

Chapter 3
All in a line

There are many occasions in the day when making a line is the safest and most orderly way of assembling the children. Informality may be your preference, so does the line benefit from organization and a particular order?

The answer is yes. A haphazard rush and crush can be dangerous, so call for a group at a time, as in *Is that my name?* (Activity 35) or *After you* (Activity 34), to stagger the formation of the line. Similarly, determine who stands where with *Filing children* (Activity 33), at the same time encouraging the children to help one another.

As everyone may not be lining up at the same time (particularly when getting changed at PE), the early arrivals will be glad of something to occupy their bodies in *At the bus stop* (Activity 37) and *Mini workout* (Activity 38), or expand their minds in *Walking dictionaries* (Activity 39).

Your aim should be to make lining-up as positive an experience as the rest of your class's day. A line may be formal, but you can still find ways to make it fun!

33. Filing children KS1, KS2

✦   Announce on Monday morning that this week you are going to file the children!

✦   Explain that alphabetical order is a common way of filing information about people; surnames are always used.

✦   Be prepared for lining up to take longer, as children gain an understanding of where there are likely to be. Have an alphabet line on display as a help.

✦   Warn them against assuming they will always be after or before the same children. What happens when some people are away? Have they still got their surname filed alphabetically now?

✦   Ring the changes one week by announcing a modern filing system: alphabetical order of first names. Make sure then you allow plenty of time for lining up!

✦   You could follow this up with *Walking filing cabinets* (Activity 40).

34. After you KS2

✦ Avoid an uncontrolled dash to be first in line for assembly by finding fun ways to vary order.

✦ Get the children thinking as you ask for children with a birthday in a month shorter than 31 days.

✦ Call for anyone whose surname starts with 'R', 'S' or 'T'.

✦ Ask for children sitting next to someone whose first name starts with 'A', 'B' or 'C'.

✦ Practise times tables by calling for children whose house or flat number is less than 9 x 3.

✦ Keep this enjoyable with quick changes of category.

35. Is that my name? KS2

✦ Use lining up to get the children thinking about spelling and phonics.

✦ Set the rules of the game: nobody can join the line until you call their 'name'.

✦ Then call for names as you are ready. For example:
1. surnames containing two vowels;
2. first names with two consonants;
3. children with a surname of one syllable;
4. anyone with a surname of more than three syllables;
5. surnames of six letters or less;
6. surnames of seven letters or more.

✦ Ring the changes by thinking of new categories every time you use this way to line up.

36. **Wakey, wakey!** KS1, KS2

✦ How wide awake were the children this morning? Did they really notice what they put on?

✦ Set a time limit for children to decide if you are describing them. If they recognize themselves too late, they have to wait for the next suitable description.

✦ Ask for:
  ◇ children wearing a hair bobble;
  ◇ those with ear-rings. (Think about this one: you may not necessarily want to know if someone is breaking school rules!)
  ◇ everyone wearing brown shoes;
  ◇ children with Velcro®- fastened shoes;
  ◇ anyone in a v-necked jumper.

✦ Obviously, avoid sensitive subjects, but use your imagination for variety and fun.

37. **At the bus stop** KS1, KS2

✦ Waiting in line is time-wasting but sometimes unavoidable. Avoid tedium with an on-the-spot exercise.

✦ On Monday morning, decide on and demonstrate a keep-fit exercise of the week: for example, 15 shoulder shrugs or trunk twists.

✦ Display a stick person diagram to remind the children of the exercise.

✦ Encourage the children to do the exercise when they join the line and wait for others.

✦ Do they feel more supple by the end of the week?

38. Mini-workout KS1, KS2

✦ Extend *At the bus stop* (Actvity 37) to a workout of the week.

✦ Display on a chart a number of exercises that can be done while staying in line.

✦ List and illustrate them in a recommended order and with a recommended number of repeats.

✦ Exercises could include:
  ✧ hand rotation;
  ✧ finger wriggle;
  ✧ fist clench-and-relax;
  ✧ knee bend;
  ✧ side-to-side weight transference;
  ✧ heel rise;
  ✧ balancing for 10 seconds on one leg.

✦ Suggest that the children try to complete a workout while they wait.

39. **Walking dictionaries** KS2

✦ Promise to turn the children into 'walking dictionaries'. It's as easy as standing in line!

✦ Make a link back to *Today's words are ...* (Activity 25) now included in the class reference glossary.

✦ Select a word that most children found difficult and write it on the whiteboard as the word of the day, with its definition.

✦ Suggest the children spend 1 minute studying the word whenever they line up during the day.

✦ By the last time they line up, can they explain its meaning to the next person in the line? Can they spell the word correctly?

Chapter 4
Changing location

There are likely to be many times in your school day when you and the children have to change location, for example moves between classroom and assembly hall, computer suite or playground. View these times as positive opportunities for the class to work as a team, as in *Target points* (Activity 41) or *Whisper, whisper* (Activity 54); to sharpen their powers of observation, as in *Where am I?* (Activity 47) and to practise their movement skills as in *Football fit!* (Activity 46).

Different situations and schools make different demands: lines in your school may be expected to keep to a particular side of the corridor, encouraged by *Target points* (Activity 41); the movement from assembly may require silence, helped when they *Walk like ... mice* (Activity 42); whereas the movement of only your class to the music room may allow for the more relaxed approach of *Humming bees* (Activity 49) or *Happy as we go!* (Activity 50).

Choose your ideas to suit the journey. Chapter 3 provided ways to make the lines; these suggestions will help the children enjoy staying in them.

40. **Walking filing cabinets** KS1, KS2

✦ Remind the children about what they did in *Filing children* (Activity 33).

✦ Suggest that they are now safely in place in the filing cabinet. The last thing you want is for the order of your files to get muddled.

✦ Challenge the children to stay in completely neat order, like files in a filing cabinet.

✦ Can they stay one exactly behind the other? The secret will be to keep their eyes fixed on the back of the head in front of them.

✦ Assess the neatness of your filing cabinet when you reach your destination. Does it merit a point towards the class target? (See *Hit the target*, Activity 6).

41. **Target points** KS1, KS2

✦ Refer to *Hit the target* (Activity 6).

✦ Announce that you have a point to give away – as long as your condition is met.

✦ Then say what the condition is, for example:
  ◇ keeping the line straight;
  ◇ all staying together;
  ◇ being very quiet;
  ◇ staying on one side of the corridor.

✦ Add on a real bribe! Announce that there will a bonus point if another teacher, a visitor or the Head praises them.

42. Walk like ... mice KS1, KS2

✦ Have a number of appealing animal pictures.

✦ Before you leave the room, hold up today's chosen animal, for example a mouse or an elephant.

✦ Stress the characteristics the children will need: the small steps, cautious movement of an inaudible mouse; the larger, steady, plodding steps of a elephant.

✦ Will a passer-by recognize what animal your class has become?

43. Cross the bridge KS1, KS2

✦ Make the move from playground to classroom more fun by using playground markings.

✦ Point out a particular line, for example the side line of the netball court.

✦ Suggest that the line is a narrow bridge. How difficult will it be to stay on it?

✦ Challenge the children to walk the full length of the bridge without falling into the water. The secret will be careful, controlled footwork.

44. **Instant growing** KS1, KS2

✦ Use this activity after PE work on movement and the correct way to hold the body.

✦ Ask the children to 'stand tall', imagining that they have a hook screwed into the top of their head and that a rope is attached to the hook lifting their head and body upwards.

✦ Now can they keep that sensation as they walk?

✦ Do they feel taller by the end of the journey? Pick out the children you think have done some instant growing!

45. D for deportment KS2

✦ What do the children know about the strict schools of the Victorian Age?

✦ Use the word deportment. Emphasize its importance in Victorian schools; the children were expected to keep their backs really straight.

✦ Ask the children to time-travel back to the Victorian Age. You, the school inspector, are here to check their deportment as they walk. Will they walk with their backs straight?

✦ Give them some tips: Instant growing and imagining a book balanced on their heads will help them.

✦ What award does the inspector give: a D for a deportment pass or a B for a board to straighten their backs?

46. Football fit! KS2

✦ Pretend the children are famous, valuable footballers.

✦ You, their team physiotherapist, are nagging them to look after their feet, ankles and knees. You do not want any more injuries!

✦ Give the children a particular, safe movement to concentrate on. For example:
  ◇ keeping knees and feet moving in line, one joint above the other;
  ◇ making sure that knees remain 'soft' not rigid;
  ◇ walking with a definite heel strike before rolling the rest of the foot down.

✦ Afterwards ask how they feel. Have they or you spotted a likely 'injury'? Are they all fit for Saturday's match?

47. **Where am I?**

✦   Use this on one of your least direct journeys.

✦   Remind the children of *Landmarks* (Activity 22).

✦   Suggest that a newcomer to the school might be making this present journey between school places on her own.

✦   As the children go along, ask them to notice and decide which one landmark would be most helpful for a newcomer to know about?

✦   Afterwards you could share ideas or let the children make a private note, ready for this afternoon's *School landmarks* (Activity 115).

48. Alliterative answers KS2

✦ Try this during a week when you are using *Funny names* (Activity 29) to answer the register.

✦ Suggest the children use a journey back to class to run through alliterative possibilities in their head for tomorrow's register.

✦ Let them jot down their ideas when they reach the classroom.

✦ They can try out their alliterative answers at home. Which one has the best sound? Will it be good enough to win tomorrow's stick-on smile?

49. Humming bees KS1, KS2

✦ Turn the children into a swarm of bees.

✦ They are the famous Bee Choir, renowned for their wonderful humming.

✦ As they stop and re-start hums, they often change musical key, so that there is an ever-changing mixture of high and low hums.

✦ Have a practice and then set off.

✦ At the end of the journey, applaud the bees for their harmonious performance.

✦ Perhaps they can provide an encore on the return journey?

50. **Happy as we go!** KS1, KS2

✦ Use this when you do not feel pressure for the children to be very quiet.

✦ Suggest raising your happiness level by having your own cheery marching song. Agree on a sensible volume.

✦ Decide on simple and easy to remember lyrics, for example:
   Hey ho! Hey ho!
   It's on our way we go.
   We keep on singing as we walk,
   Hey ho! Hey ho!

✦ As the singing line makes its way, move up and down it, leading the singing and helping voices keep together.

51. **Observation!** KS2

✦ Tell the children that they are going to play a game of Observation!

✦ Explain that when they reach their destination, you will ask them three to five questions connected with the journey.

✦ The questions might be linked to people, things or places. For example:
   ✧ Who was the teacher we passed in the corridor?
   ✧ What was the title of the display in the entrance hall?
   ✧ Where was there a stack of chairs?

✦ Journey times will whizz by as the children learn to keep their eyes peeled!

52. Quizmaster KS2

✦ Remind the children about *Observation!* (Activity 51).

✦ Announce that today, when they reach their destination, they will have the chance to reverse roles: they will be the quizmaster, you will answer the questions.

✦ They have to use the journey to prepare one or two questions.

✦ In your new location, put the children into groups of four to share ideas and agree on questions likely to fox you.

✦ If possible, answer a question from each group.

✦ How do the children rate your observation skills?

53. Look out! KS1, KS2

✦ Ask the children to act as health and safety inspectors, doing a patrol of this part of the school.

✦ As they walk, the children should be alert for proof of the school's health and safety awareness. (Tidiness; warning sign of a wet floor; clean windows; swept floors and paths.)

✦ They will also be watching for negative points and potential hazards (litter; coats on the floor; a box for someone to trip over; mud on the path to slip on).

✦ At the end of the journey, agree on the grade the inspectors will award.

✦ Are there problems the children can do something about?

54. **Whisper, whisper** KS1, KS2

✦ Tell the children that you are going to show them how strange rumours can spread.

✦ Set the rules of the game:
  ✧ whispering not talking;
  ✧ whispering the message once only.

✦ Whisper a short message to the child at the end of the line. For example:
  It's double toast for lunch.

✦ Go to the front of the line.

✦ Ask the child at the back of the line to whisper the message to the person ahead of them.

✦ The children must continue to pass the message along the line, keeping their voice to a whisper so only the person in front can hear.

✦ When the message is passed to you, stop the line and repeat what you think you have heard.

✦ Compare this with the message you gave. How different are they? (If necessary, cheat by making sure that you 'hear' a faulty message, for example: There's a dreaded test for literacy.)

✦ From now on, whispered secrets will never be trusted!

Chapter 5
Starting the afternoon

Starting the afternoon can be the most difficult transition time of the day. The lunch break is long; younger children may have become tired and tearful; older children may have become cross, argued with classmates or got into trouble with lunch supervisors. Some children are over-excited; some children have been bored and lonely. Everyone needs help in re-adjusting to the atmosphere of the classroom.

Try to provide an activity that the children can immediately settle to. Many of these ideas, such as *Stress-buster* (Activity 73) and *Musical inspirations* (Activity 64) are calming. Knowing about an activity in advance affords a similarly smooth transition: for example, a week spent on flags for *Let's go to …* (Activity 59) or on letters for *Dear Ed …* (Activity 58).

Think about accommodating the class's current needs. Lunchtime behaviour may have become a problem: *Afternoon blog* (Activity 60) and *Time for everything* (Activity 55) encourage the children to analyse their use of the break. Make your idea fit the day. A wet day with no access to outdoor play may leave the children ready to enjoy the humour of *That's a funny story!* (Activity 71) or the practical revision of the song and exercises behind *Marching songs* and *Still waiting for that bus!* (Activities 68 and 70).

55. **Time for everything** KS1, KS2

✦ After the hustle and bustle of lunchtime, give the children time to reflect on everything they have been doing during break.

✦ Explain that you want them to help future new children to make best use of the school lunch break.

✦ New children will need a timetable, advising them what to do when.

✦ As the children create one, emphasize the need to help the newcomer to have as enjoyable a lunchtime as possible while still doing everything they need to. (For younger children, representation could be pictorial.)

56. **Eat well!**   KS1, KS2

✦   Give some thinking time as the children remember and list what they have eaten this lunchtime.

✦   It would be fun for them to draw a plate of these food items, perhaps dividing the plate into foods that go together.

✦   Older children should be able to link their plates to science work on healthy eating, with the plate divided into food group sections: fruit and vegetables, carbohydrates, proteins and fats.

✦   Do this for the whole week, the children labelling each plate drawing with its day.

57. **Balanced eaters**   KS1, KS2

✦   At the end of the week, follow up *Eat well!* (Activity 56).

✦   Do the children think they are really eating well?

✦   Encourage them to look carefully at the balance of their plates, asking themselves:
    ◇ Is one food group doing badly?
    ◇ Should I try to increase some foods next week?
    ◇ Is there anything I should try to have less of?

✦   Suggest they make a brief oral report of their findings to a partner and make a written note of their resolutions.

58. Dear Ed ...

✦ Put a postcard-size piece of paper at every place.

✦ Remind the children what a wise and reliable friend Ed, the class teddy, is.

✦ Ask the children to think if they have any suggestions, problems or worries they want to send to Ed.

✦ Alternatively, they may have noticed another child's particularly helpful action they think should be recognized.

✦ Suggest they may prefer to write anonymously.

✦ Have a Suggestion box in which the children can place these letters throughout the week.

59. **Let's go to ...** KS1, KS2

✦ Hold a tourism week and treat everyone to some relaxing colouring.

✦ Create, by hand or computer, and photocopy some blank flags.

✦ Each day announce a visit to a different country: Italy, France, Germany or Spain.

✦ Do the children know the country's flag? Help them find out. (The information will be readily accessible in a reference book or on the Internet.)

✦ Give out blank flags for the children to draw and colour today's flag, writing the country's name on the back.

✦ Promise the children a game with their set of flags at the end of the week *Fly the flag* (Activity 123).

60. Afternoon blog   KS2

✦ Do the children know the term blog? Explain that it is an on-line, personal diary, one's own thoughts and ideas.

✦ Point out that the lunchtime play session is the longest of the day.

✦ Suggest the children write a short blog at the beginning of every afternoon this week, recording their thoughts about that day's lunchtime.

✦ Suggest questions they may want to ask themselves:
  ✧ Did you get enough exercise during lunchtime today?
  ✧ Have you overtired yourself?
  ✧ Do you think you should have included more people in your games?
  ✧ Is there something you want to do differently tomorrow?

✦ They can write it by hand, but may enjoy transferring it to computer at some later stage.

61. Fishy folk   KS1, KS2

✦ Show the children some pictures of fish. Emphasize the variety of shape, colour and pattern.

✦ Tell the children you want them to draw their own fish and give them time to think about their own personal design.

✦ Give out white paper for the children to draw and colour their special, fishy species.

✦ Ask them to cut out their fish, put their name on the back, and save it for *Pond challenge* (Activity 94).

62. **Clever clues** KS2

✦ Use this idea as a follow-on in the afternoon to *Clues to the past* (Activity 15).

✦ Give the children the opportunity to re-read their clues to remind themselves who they want to be.

✦ Ask them to review each clue:
  ✧ Does it lead to their identity?
  ✧ Is one too obvious?
  ✧ Can they now think of a clever replacement?

✦ Suggest they number the clues, number 1 being the cleverest, number 10 the most obvious.

✦ Promise to use the clues at the end of the day in a game of *Who am I?* (Activity 120).

63. **Picture the food** KS2, KS2

✦ Admit that you are already thinking about food again!

✦ Ask the children to let their thoughts drift to after school and what they are likely to eat today.

✦ Ask them to draw the plate of food they expect to have and label the foods.

✦ Draw and label your own plate of food, perhaps bearing in mind some of your register time promises! (See *Talking food*, Activity 27.)

✦ Keep the plates safe for a fun language activity in *Time for tea!* (Activity 122).

64. Musical inspirations

KS1, KS2

✦ Have a musical focus for the week: a single work (for example, The Four Seasons); one composer (for example, Vivaldi); music related to a theme (for example, changes in nature).

✦ Have the music on as the children enter the room. Let them sit, listen and enjoy.

✦ Afterwards, encourage the children to exchange reactions with a partner. Did they enjoy the music? What mood did it inspire in them?

✦ Tell the children a little about the music: where the extract is from and the name of the composer.

✦ Make this an enjoyable way to broaden the children's musical knowledge and experience, and give them the confidence to voice their opinions.

65. **What will I say?**   KS2

✦   Do this when you plan to end your day with *The big conversation* (Activity 113). Look at its format.

✦   Tell the children what you plan to discuss, for example healthy eating.

✦   Write on the whiteboard two of your planned conversation item questions related to healthy eating.

✦   Ask the children to think about their answers. What points will they make?

✦   Suggest they jot down notes in readiness for the discussion later.

The Eatwell Plate

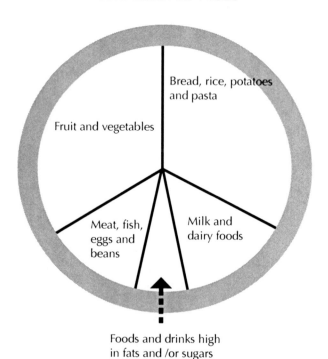

Bread, rice, potatoes and pasta

Fruit and vegetables

Meat, fish, eggs and beans

Milk and dairy foods

Foods and drinks high in fats and /or sugars

66. **Picture the story** KS2

✦ You are concerned that a KS1 class may visit! You want to have some suitable stories ready. Can the children help you?

✦ Point out that young children respond well to pictures, so you want them to create a story in pictures.

✦ Give everyone a photocopied storyboard, with boxes for their pictures. (Make sure there is space left under each box.)

✦ Recommend using a setting familiar to young children (the home, shops or school).

✦ They need to keep their picture story for tomorrow's activity, *Add the words* (Actvity 67).

67. **Add the words** KS2

✦   Remind the children of their *Picture the story* (previous activity) storyboards.

✦   Explain that you have learned that the visitors can read short simple sentences.

✦   Emphasize the importance of choosing vocabulary carefully, as the children write a sentence beneath each picture.

✦   Bring reality to your idea by inviting a younger class to your classroom. Let everyone share their book with a visitor. That way, they will see how much it is enjoyed, and be on hand to help with any reading or story comprehension problems.

68. **Marching songs** KS1, KS2

✦ Remind the children of the way they sometimes sing as they move from place to place *Happy as we go!* (Activity 50).

✦ Suggest that you really need a new marching song.

✦ Remind them of a successful one, perhaps the example in *Happy as we go!* (Activity 50).

✦ Set some restrictions for their songwriting:

   ✧ four lines;

   ✧ the words of the new song must be catchy so they will be remembered easily.

✦ Let the children see what they can come up with. You could help by writing an optional starting line on the whiteboard. For example:
One, two! One, two!

✦ Save them for the end of the afternoon (*Let's sing*, Activity 126).

69. **Lost for words!** KS2

✦ Make this activity relevant to literacy work, asking the children to write in the style of a fable.

✦ Confess your problem. You have started writing your own fable, but have run out of ideas. Can the children finish writing it.

✦ Display your story start. For example:

Cat was always chasing Mouse.
He made her life so miserable
she was becoming afraid to take a walk.
One day she had an idea …

✦ Emphasize that you want the story to be short, so set a time limit of five to ten minutes.

✦ Challenge the children to add a moral to the story.

✦ These stories will make wonderful texts for a future literacy lesson.

70. **Still waiting for that bus!** KS1, KS2

✦ Remind the children of recent *At the bus stop* exercises the class has been using (see Activity 37).

✦ Admit you are running out of new ideas.

✦ Ask for the children's help in supplying a new exercise, perhaps just a slight variation of one of your ideas. They need to write an explanation and show how to do the exercise in a clear stick-person diagram.

✦ Some children may have enough ideas to work out a new *Mini-workout* (Activity 38).

✦ Suggest saving notes and diagrams until the end of the afternoon.

71. **That's a funny story!** KS2

✦ Tell the children that at the end of one afternoon this week you plan to hold a storytelling session. The children will be the storytellers!

✦ Explain that you want to make the session fun, so you are looking for short, light-hearted stories.

✦ Put the children into twos, give each pair a piece of paper on which you have written an intriguing story opener. The partners must decide how to continue the story – good openers are:

  ✧ You're never going to believe this …

  ✧ It all started with …

  ✧ A funny thing happened on my way to …

  ✧ Everything seemed to be going well until …

  ✧ Things always go wrong on a …

  ✧ It was not funny at the time but …

✦ Let partners collaborate as they work out and write their story, using note form, not complete sentences. (Some children may prefer to work independently.)

✦ Use *It's storytime* (Activities 132–133) shortly after this activity.

72. **What's my cue?** KS2

✦ Remind the children of how you told your story in *It's storytime* (Activities 132–133).

✦ Show the children the cue cards you used. Point out they are in a numbered sequence and have very few words on them. (One cue card could be a picture only.)

✦ Emphasize that they have just enough to remind you of the next part of your story.

✦ Let partners refresh their memories for their funny stories from *That's a funny story!* (Activity 71).

✦ Give them six to eight postcard size pieces of card to make their cue cards.

✦ Save the completed cue cards for the end of the day.

73. **Stress-buster** KS1, KS2

✦ You feel stressed! Tell the children you have had a hard morning.

✦ Explain that you sometimes find looking at an appropriate picture has a calming effect on you.

✦ Challenge them to draw and colour a picture that will be an instant stress-buster. What will they need to think about? (For example, the colour, scene or happenings.)

✦ Save the pictures for tomorrow's *How does it work?* (Activity 74).

74. How does it work?

✦ Tell the children that you are still feeling stressed. Remind them of their pictures from yesterday's *Stress-buster* (Activity 73).

✦ Ask them to write a paragraph about their picture.

✦ Suggest questions to put to themselves:
  ✧ What should help someone looking at my picture relax?
  ✧ Why will it have that effect?
  ✧ What is particularly important?

✦ Do a test: when the children hold up their pictures, does your stress melt away?

Chapter 6
Circle time

Circle time may differ from school to school: its length; its time of day; and its frequency during the week. Nevertheless, for all, it should be a wonderful opportunity to unite the class in bonding activities, such as *Shipwreck survivors* (Activity 88) and to sort out class problems, as in *We have a problem!* and *Find a solution!* (Activities 80 and 81).

Circle time also cares for the individual. From *The magic talk box* (Activity 75) through to *Pipedreams* (Activity 89), the children can gain the confidence to share their own thoughts and to listen respectfully to others. *Well done!* (Activity 98) is their deserved chance for an individual moment of glory.

Finally, think about really forming the circle shape. It lends itself to *All at sea* (Activity 86) and *Parachute fun* (Activity 87) and demonstrates visually the values of working together. The circle's shape also encourages you all, as in *Follow that story …* (Activity 79) and *All in a ring* (Activity 96), to just have fun!

75. **The magic talk box** KS1, KS2

✦ This is a good activity at the start of the year. It empowers less confident speakers and establishes a pattern of listening to one another.

✦ Show the children a small, attractive box. Explain that it is your magic talk box: whoever is holding it has the power of speech and everyone else always listens.

✦ Suggest that it is really time to introduce yourselves!

✦ Hold the box as you introduce yourself to the circle: your name and some further details, perhaps about your family and interests.

✦ Let the children pass the box round the circle as they each make their introduction.

Hello, my name is Rashid, and I like...

76. **I never knew that!** KS1, KS2

◆ Remind the children of their introductions in *The magic talk box* (Activity 75). You think they have many interesting parts to their lives!

◆ Suggest a topic for conversation, relating it to out-of-school life, for example the weekend or after-school hobbies.

◆ Ask the children to have paired talks with the person next to them in the circle.

◆ Pass the talk box around as children prove what good listeners they are by repeating something new or interesting they have found out about the person sitting next to them.

77. **Discovery of the week** KS1, KS2

◆ This would be a good activity for Thursday or Friday.

◆ Ask the children to think about this week's time at school.

◆ Jog their memories by reminding them of topic areas, assembly themes and special happenings.

◆ Give thinking time as the children decide what they have learned this week. What do they want to pick out?

◆ Use the talk box as the children tell the circle of their discovery of the week.

78. **Spot the chief** KS1, KS2

✦ Select one person, the Scout, from the circle. Ask them to leave the room.

✦ With the Scout gone, choose another child as Chief: he or she will start movements for the others to copy. Movements will change very often, but only the Chief can start the changes and knows what they will be.

✦ The rest of the circle must try to keep the Chief's identity secret, so their watching cannot be too obvious.

✦ When the missing child returns, the circle, led by the Chief, begins some movements (shrugging shoulders, clapping, clicking fingers, tapping the nose).

✦ Ask the Scout to return. Using sharp powers of observation, how long will it take the Scout to identify the Chief? Set a time limit and restrict the number of guesses before the circle reveals its Chief.

✦ Play a new game with new children in the roles of Scout and Chief.

79. **Follow that story ...** KS2

✦ Suggest the circle have fun by creating a story to which everyone can contribute.

✦ You begin with an opening sentence, for example
It was late afternoon when Coco, the children's entertainer, arrived nervously at the school Christmas party.

✦ Move around the circle as everyone adds a sentence. Keep the atmosphere light-hearted and avoid putting pressure on children who find this activity difficult by letting the story move quickly to the next person.

✦ Do this a few times, with you beginning new stories. Contributions will become more imaginative and children will feel confident that mistakes are impossible.

✦ Which story would they like to see in print?

80. We have a problem! KS2

✦ Every class encounters problems and they often benefit from discussion.

✦ Suggest that Ed, the class teddy, has heard about an issue affecting your class. He wants to know why it is happening.

✦ Encourage children to talk about why the problem exists, letting them show by gesture when they would like to use the talk box.

✦ Use your own talk box interventions to model a calm, reasonable approach.

✦ Let Ed, (via you) sum up at the end what he has heard.

81. Find the solution! KS2

✦ Refer to *We have a problem!* (previous activity) and remind the circle of the points made.

✦ Ed has now requested a solution.

✦ Resume the discussion as children make their suggestions.

✦ Use your own talk box interventions to model respecting different viewpoints and reaching compromises.

✦ Agree on a solution and pass the message to Ed.

✦ Suggest that it could be helpful to write the class's agreement down in a special book.

82. **Classroom code (part 1)** KS2

✦ Ask the circle to think about what matters most to them in classroom life. Can they sum it up in one word?

✦ Brainstorm some answers. Focus on one or two (for example, happiness and belonging) and discuss how to ensure that the classroom and everyone's behaviour provide them.

✦ Suggest that a classroom code of conduct, which everyone aims to respect, would be a good idea.

✦ After partner collaboration, listen to some of the points suggested by the children. Make a note of them for another day.

83. **Classroom code (part 2)** KS2

✦ Review the suggestions from the previous activity.

✦ In discussion, collaborate on re-wording some of the points so they are positive rather than negative.

✦ How many points should the code make? Are there any suggestions the children now feel should be left out? What about including the result from *Find the solution!* (Activity 81).

✦ Produce a final Code of Conduct for permanent display to remind everyone what is expected of them.

84. **Pass the question parcel** KS2

✦ Make a question cube, on which you write about four to six questions. Cover each question with a peel-off flap.

✦ Keep the questions to one theme, for example happiness.
   ✧ What always makes you happy?
   ✧ How do you show you are happy?
   ✧ What has been your happiest moment today?
   ✧ How do you try to make others happy?

✦ Follow the format of the party game, 'Pass the parcel' with music playing as the parcel is passed around the circle.

✦ When the music stops, whoever is holding the cube peels off a flap to reveal the question and reads it out.

✦ Use the question for a mixture of partner talk and circle answers.

✦ Other interesting question themes are kindness, difficulties and sharing.

85. Catch this mood!

KS1, KS2

✦ Adopt body language showing a clear mood, perhaps slumped shoulders or pursed lips. Ask the circle how they think you are feeling. Are they correct? How are they affected?

✦ Suggest that our facial expressions and body language often reveal our feelings. Other people may even catch our moods.

✦ Play a partner game, in which the children think of an emotion and a situation that inspires that emotion in them. They must let their face and body show the feeling. Can their partner tell how they are feeling? How does the mood appear to the watcher? Is the watcher's own mood affected?

✦ Continue the game, partners taking turns with roles. Encourage the children to work through a range of moods.

✦ Finish with the whole circle displaying one mood, for example enthusiasm. Are the children able to pass the mood on to you?

86. **All at sea**

✦ Have creative fun, yet team-build at the same time.

✦ You will need a large, preferably circular, piece of blue material (perhaps your best tablecloth!) and a simple poem about the sea.

✦ Make sure the poem describes the sea in different states – rough, calm, stormy, still. If you don't want to write your own poem, lines from *Waves* by Jackie Kay work well.

✦ Read the poem aloud, making sure that the children can identify the sea's changes.

✦ Place the material inside the circle, asking all the children to hold its edge.

✦ This time bring the poem to life: you read it as the children transform the blue material into a sea that matches the current words of the poem. In order to make the sea realistic, the circle must work together.

87. **Parachute fun** KS1, KS2

✦ If your PE equipment includes a parachute, it is a wonderful resource for circle time.

✦ Use a large space – outside or the hall – and become a weather forecaster.

✦ Explain that you will be reporting weather from all over the world, so the children must be prepared for anything.

✦ As they stand holding the parachute, call out different conditions: breezy, hurricane, heavy rain, soft snow, typhoon. Let the circle watch and respond to one another's movements as they work together to create collaborative weather pictures.

88. **Shipwreck survivors** KS2

✦ Set the scenario: you have all been shipwrecked and washed up on a desert island. To manage, you need to work together.

✦ Pass around the talk box, as children suggest essential actions you need to take.

✦ Suggest that it will be better to share out tasks, perhaps working in groups. Ask the children to think about their own and other people's qualities and skills.

✦ Speaking again, let the children suggest people – themselves or others – for particular roles and tasks.

✦ Help the children to recognize the value of everyone's contribution to life on the desert island.

89. Pipe-dreams KS1, KS2

✦ Everyone has impossible pipedreams. Tell the children yours: I think I could be the fastest runner at the Olympic Games.

✦ Admit that you know this is really impossible, as you are not even good at running!

✦ Let the children dream up fanciful ambitions and share them with the circle.

✦ When your turn to speak comes again, declare another ambition, this time more realistic. For example: **"I may become Head Teacher of a big school."**

✦ Let the circle take turns speaking again, sharing their ambitions.

✦ Finally, make your last hope reflect your current situation. For example, I want the other teachers to look more pleased with my assemblies.

✦ The circle's final comments can offer you and the children insights into the needs of others.

90. **Making improvements** KS2

✦ Refer to *Afternoon blog* (Activity 60).

✦ Reveal that you have written your own blog. Read it to the children.

✦ Use your magic talk box to organize discussion of comments on your blog. Does your lunchtime sound happy? Can the children suggest how you can improve tomorrow's lunchtime? How can you make sure you are not overtired?

✦ Let volunteers share their blogs with close neighbours in the circle.

✦ Encourage the listeners to suggest ways for the readers to improve lunchtime.

✦ Finish with the whole circle agreeing on a class resolution that could make lunchtime a better play session for everyone.

91. Toss the rhyme

KS1, KS2

✦ You will need Ed and a small soft ball.

✦ The children can play as individuals or in twos or threes.

✦ Begin with you and Ed in control of the ball. With your voice, let Ed say a simple word.

✦ Then toss the ball to someone else. That person or group needs to say a rhyming word and toss the ball on.

✦ When a rhyming sequence seems to have reached an end, Ed and you can resume control of the ball and begin a different rhyme.

✦ Keep the starting words simple, and perhaps have some words on display so that the whole circle finds the game fast-moving and fun.

92. **Soothometer** KS1, KS2

✦ Try this after stressful mornings!

✦ Remind the children of their pictures and writing from *Stressbuster* and *How does it work?* (Activities 73 and 74).

✦ Give the children the chance to present and talk about their pictures to a partner.

✦ Ask the circle to imagine feeling tense and nervous. Children can take turns holding up their soothing pictures, while the viewers use their fingers and thumbs to register a soothometer score.

✦ Which picture wins the day?

✦ Display the pictures as a mood wall. Whenever life gets too much, the children can face it!

93. A is for ...

✦ Play the alphabet game, choosing a topic such as animals and plants.

✦ Decide on a gesture, perhaps raising a hand, to indicate who is ready to take the talk box and contribute the next alphabet letter's animal or plant.

✦ Avoid fast thinkers dominating the game by various means, for example:
  ✧ At least three alphabet letters must pass before you can have the talk box again;
  ✧ Children can collaborate with a partner;
  ✧ Ed may slyly help people who are stuck by pointing to a picture.

✦ As you exhaust one topic, move to others such as first names, classroom objects, UK towns and villages, and countries of the world.

✦ Make sure Ed's contributions keep the game fun.

94. **Pond challenge**   **KS1, KS2**

✦   You will need one large piece of blue paper or card and pencils, crayons and felt tips for everyone.

✦   Place the sheet of paper on the floor and suggest that it could make an ideal home for the children's fish from *Fishy folk* (Activity 61). Unfortunately, it still looks like a piece of blue paper!

✦   Set a time limit of five to ten minutes, challenging the children to make the environment more realistic by drawing and colouring the pond's edge.

✦   Encourage everyone to do their best to colour in their part of the perimeter but they may help a neighbour if in difficulty.

✦   Afterwards, congratulate the children on their wonderful team effort; move the pond to a display area; and let the children put their fish in.

95. **Hear the signs**   KS1, KS2

✦ Introduce your children to the important world of sign language. Teach them some simple signs: hello, I, you, thank you, good, goodbye, are all straightforward possibilities.

✦ Read the children a short story, signing these words when you reach them.

✦ Draw and display pictures of the signs.

✦ Now read the story a second time and let the circle take responsibility for making the signs.

96. **All in a ring** KS1

✦ Introduce the children to this nursery rhyme:

Here we go 'round the mulberry bush,
The mulberry bush,
The mulberry bush,
Here we go 'round the mulberry bush,
So early in the morning.

✦ All link hands as you skip round in a circle, singing it.

✦ Suggest adding new verses, in which the mulberry bush is changed to something else. (For example, the Christmas tree; the maypole stand; the blackberry bush.)

✦ Dance around to the new verses, retaining the last line of the original verse.

✦ Finish with the ever-popular Ring a Ring o' Roses. Make sure that everyone helps their neighbour up after they all fall down.

97. **Ed says ...** KS1, KS2

✦ Remind yourself of *Dear Ed* (Activity 58), and investigate this week's mail.

✦ In Friday's circle time sit Ed on a chair beside you.

✦ Ask Ed to read out (through your voice) some problems written to him this week.

✦ Discuss the problems as a circle. Agree on advice to offer the anonymous writer.

✦ Be ready to 'plant' your own letter in the box in order to focus attention on a current issue.

98. **Well done!** KS1, KS2

✦ Use Friday's circle time for a private, end-of-week, class assembly.

✦ Ask individual children to stand up as you talk about achievements that have pleased Ed (and you) this week – perhaps gaining a first swimming certificate, or being especially helpful to classmates.

✦ Let the circle give these children the applause they deserve.

✦ Then enter their names in your special Well done! book. Children and parents will take great pleasure from seeing names there.

✦ Occasionally, hold this short assembly at the end of Friday afternoon and share it with parents. It makes a lovely end to the week.

Chapter 7
Changing lesson

Changing lesson can be a particularly difficult afternoon transition time. Many schools have dispensed with an afternoon break, yet curriculum needs necessitate a lesson change. Movement to a new location brings the first half of the afternoon to a natural end, but without that you must look for other ways to help the children make the transition.

If the children have been involved in a lesson with intense focus, such as history research on Tudor exploration, play a light-hearted game, such as *Guesstimate* (Activity 100). This will allow the children to 'file' what they have just been doing and clear their minds for a new curriculum focus.

The afternoon lesson change is likely to coincide with the body's natural dip in energy. Acknowledge this, as in *Recharge the brain battery* (Activity 99), or the first part of *Switch off! Swith on!* (Activity 104). Explain the debilitating effect of dehydration and encourage the children to drink water. Have they been sitting for a long time? Suggest that exercise will raise their energy levels, as they move to Switch on! or prepare to be *On the catwalk* or just *Take five!* (Activities 105 and 107).

If you have time and space, the active fun of *Square dancing* (Activity 106) will ensure that brains and bodies are definitely re-energized and prepared for the challenges of the rest of the day!

99. **Recharge the brain battery** KS1, KS2

✦ When the children seem sluggish during the afternoon, suggest their brain batteries need recharging! Will some brain gym exercises help?

✦ Ask the children to watch as you turn your back on the class and write your name in the air. Can they read what you have written?

✦ Let the children stand up and use the forefinger of their dominant hand to write their own name in the air. Can they add a family member's name? Can someone else read it?

✦ Demonstrate how the brain co-ordinates thinking, as you pat your head with one hand, while your other hand rubs your stomach in small circles. How good are the children at doing this? Swap hands!

Changing lessons

100. **Guesstimate** KS1, KS2

✦   Unwind between lessons with a game of Guesstimate.

✦   Show the children a transparent container of objects, for example coloured counters or multifix pieces.

✦   After brief observation, the children must guess the number of items in the jar. Ask them to write their estimate on a piece of paper.

✦   Together, count the contents of the jar.

✦   Compare the actual number with the estimates. Was anyone spot on? Reward them with bonus house points, useful for the class target *Hit the target* (Activity 6).

✦   Vary Guesstimate by asking for estimates of units of measurement. For an end of week game, consider counting sweets. A sweet each will make you all ready for the next lesson!

101. Follow on KS2

✦ Prepare a set of number cards, each with two sections. The main section has a sum or question, for example 4 x 5. Above the question is the answer section, for example 10. It is important that the question and answer do not match.

✦ Give a card to each child.

✦ Ask someone to stand up and read out their question. If someone else has the matching answer, they can stand up and read it out. If correct, the game continues with the answerer reading out their question.

✦ Keep the game fast-moving, by making the cards suit the children's current numeracy work.

102. Word associations KS1, KS2

✦ Have fun as you play a silly word game.

✦ Tell the children that they are going to say the first word to come into their head after they have heard a word.

✦ Decide on the order of speakers (perhaps stand in a horseshoe shape) and emphasize the need to say a word quickly in order not to break the chain. (You could have a time limit of a few seconds.)

✦ Now you start the game, perhaps with the word 'party'.

✦ Make a note of the funniest associations, and on the whiteboard write down your starting and finishing words.

✦ When the chain breaks down, begin a new one. Other good starting words could be jelly, wand, snowball or sandcastle.

103. **Pleased to meet you** KS1, KS2

✦ Hold an impromptu party between lessons!

✦ Set the scenario of a social gathering in which everyone is a stranger to everyone else; nevertheless, they all want to be friendly and chat.

✦ Ask the children to walk around, wandering from person to person, as they hold conversations. They will need to introduce themselves. How will they seem friendly? What will they talk about? Can they make sure they show interest in the other person?

✦ At the end, ask them about their most sociable chat.

104. Switch off! Switch on! KS1, KS2

✦ Suggest the children forget all about the work they have been doing.

✦ Let the children act out the scene you describe:
  ◈ Off: You are lying in a corner of the school field. The weather is sunny and you are feeling pleasantly warm and relaxed. You do not have a care in the world. Now you glance at your watch ... .
  ◈ On: Look at the time! 2.25! You shake yourself awake. You leap up, put on shoes and socks, smooth your hair, grab your school bag, race into class and sit down.

✦ Phew! The next lesson is just about to begin.

105. **On the catwalk**

✦ Announce that today is the day of the end-of-term fashion show; all the famous designers and buyers will be there.

✦ The students (the children) need to rest before the frantic rush: when the alarm bell rings they will be getting ready to dress and model their own design.

✦ Let the children slouch in their chairs to rest. Then ring the alarm, so they jump up and start. Call out occasional, urgent prompts as they mime getting ready. For example:
  ✧ Your hair needs combing! How will it stay in place?
  ✧ What about make up?
  ✧ You've forgotten that zip! There's a button undone!
  ✧ Check your clothes in a mirror.
  ✧ Practise your walk.
  ✧ Now down the catwalk you go.

✦ It would be fun to treat this first attempt as a rehearsal; add lively music; and try the whole scene again.

106. Square dancing KS2

✦ Announce that it is square dance time!

✦ Take the role of caller, as you call out the dance moves. For example:
  ◈ Make a four and form a square.
  ◈ Walking right off you go.
  ◈ Change direction to the left.
  ◈ Standing still, clap your hands.
  ◈ Click your fingers good and loud.
  ◈ Face a partner in your square.
  ◈ Skip across and swap that place.
  ◈ Now skip alone around the room.
  ◈ And off you go and start again …
  ◈ Make a four and form a square.
  ◈ Walking right … (Repeat lines as before, the children now in new squares).

✦ The children will find this activity fun and enjoy repeating it on other days. As it becomes familiar, surprise them with new instructions and moves.

107. Take five!

✦ Suggest that you all need some physical exercise in order to tackle the rest of the day.

✦ Return to *At the bus stop* (Activity 37).

✦ Let the children practise the exercise of the week.

✦ Move to the complete workout of *Mini-workout* (Activity 38).

✦ If there is energy left, finish with five star jumps.

✦ After all that, everyone will definitely be fit for the next subject!

108. Opposites

KS2

✦ Tell the children they are going to sharpen their thinking in a game of Opposites.

✦ Give an example: For example:
What is the opposite of sharp? (Answer: blunt.)

✦ Give everyone a piece of paper or their individual whiteboard. Ask them to write a question for the game, trying to make it one that might beat other people. After writing the answer underneath, they put their paper face down in front of them.

✦ Choose someone to stand as the first questioner. Set a condition, for example:
   ✧ Ask a girl with long, dark hair.
   ✧ Ask a boy in the school football team.

✦ If the child asked answers correctly, they now stand and the questioner sits.

✦ Continue in this way, each time setting a condition for how the questioner chooses the person to ask.

✦ A winner is someone whose question is not answered correctly. List winners on the whiteboard and award them special house points. If the game produces only one winner award a Champion of the day sticker.

Chapter 8

The end of the day

The end of the day is the time to bring the children together; to reinforce their feeling of being one class; and to remind them of their important place in it. Inclusive activities, such as *Target totals* (Activity 109) and *Clocking-off* (Activity 112) do this, fostering strong whole-class spirit, yet bolstering self-esteem.

Consider the day the children have had. Finish a particularly tiring day with *Time to relax* (Activity 130) before moving to *Who's that on the carpet?* (Activity 116) or all joining in *Interactive story fun* (Activity 110). After a wet day inside or a quiet day of SATs, use ideas such as *Let's sing!* and *Music time* (Activities 126 and 128) for a release of noise and feelings.

The children will recognize that not every day is perfect. Let them express their feelings, admitting mistakes, problems and disappointments. Nevertheless, progress to optimism as in *Hotel satisfaction* and *How was your day?* (Activities 111 and 129). This way, the children will leave with the confidence that they can improve tomorrow.

As with morning arrival, the end of the day is the immediate bridge between school and home. The final impression of school is as important as the morning's first: one will affect the other. Your aim, as captured well by *See you again!* (Activity 119) must be that every child will look forward to tomorrow's return.

Finally, have fun! This is a wonderful time for games, as the children make the transition from the work of the day to the leisure of home. *Changing teachers* and *I-spy with a difference!* (Activities 121 and 131) successfully bridge that gap.

109. **Target totals** KS1, KS2

✦ Remind the children about the class target *Hit the target* (Activity 6).

✦ Each day, tot up your figures from the corner of the whiteboard and fill in the the week's chart.

✦ Ask the children to check the week's target. Do they think the class is going to reach it? What will happen if they win this number of points every day? Do they need to increase their daily average?

✦ Wipe clean the corner of the whiteboard ready for another day.

✦ At the end of the week, do the final totting up. Remember: no prize unless the target is hit!

✦ If the class misses the target, discuss where and how to improve their chances next week.

110. Interactive story fun KS1, KS2

✦ Choose a short home-time story with five or six repeated speaking parts. (You can re-write a story.)

✦ Using colour coding, write the speaking parts on the whiteboard. Have one coloured cube for each colour.

✦ Divide the class into the appropriate number of groups for the number of speaking parts. Assign each group a colour.

✦ Let groups practise their words before you try out the story.

✦ Read the story aloud. As you reach words to be spoken, hold up the appropriate cube, a group's cue to say their words.

✦ Hold a rehearsal before your final interactive story reading.

111. Hotel satisfaction KS1, KS2

✦ Return to your hotel scenario *Hotel guests* (Activity 2), asking the guests to re-read their early morning forms.

✦ They need to consider what they wrote and ask themselves if they have achieved their aims.

✦ Ask them to record their thoughts now in the second section of their form.

✦ Afterwards, write this question on the whiteboard: How can you make school better for yourself tomorrow?

✦ The children should write their answer in the form's third section. (For younger children, representation could be pictorial.)

✦ Each day follow the same early morning (Hotel guests) and end-of-day (Hotel satisfaction) routine, as the children complete a new form. At the end of the week, staple together the five pages.

✦ Do they think they are leaving on Friday as satisfied hotel guests? Has each day been better than the last?

112. Clocking off KS1, KS2

✦ Remind the children of the jobs they did for you this morning *Help wanted!* (Activity 10).

✦ Is there an obvious reversal or completion process? (Computers may need switching off; pencil pots may need removing from tables; your evening's marking could be placed in the collection basket so you remember to take it home; the bookcase may need a final tidying).

✦ Ask children to complete the day's job before 'clocking off' by handing in their job card.

✦ All sit down and relax before the children go, giving you time to thank the children for their voluntary help!

113. The big conversation KS2

✦ Choose a conversation topic of the week, perhaps matching an assembly theme or curriculum area, such as healthy eating.

✦ Break the topic into five conversation items and list them as questions on the whiteboard. For example: Have you eaten a balanced diet today? Which food type have you not eaten enough of?

✦ Ask the children to discuss a conversation item with a partner. Increase self-confidence by keeping these discussions short, so that children are not at a loss for things to say. After one minute, you could call 'All change', signalling the children to move to the next item or even to new talk partners.

✦ After a few weeks of partner discussion, the children will be better speakers and listeners, ready for group and then a grand class conversation.

114. **Time management**

✦   Remind the children of this morning's *What a rush!* (Activity 3).

✦   Ask the children to look at the data they noted about their morning before school. How much time did they have? How much did they have to do?

✦   Can they spot where they were rushed? Where could they save time?

✦   Ask them to produce a timetable for themselves for tomorrow morning's pre-school routine – one that they think will work well.

✦   Suggest that when they arrive tomorrow, they should record how their timetable has failed or succeeded. (Ticks, crosses and notes would work well.)

✦   Making alterations to the planned timetable each afternoon, and assessing success the following morning would be an interesting and useful week's investigation.

115. School landmarks KS2

✦ Remind the children of *Landmarks* (Activity 22).

✦ Repeat your comments about a map helping other people's understanding of where a journey's landmark is.

✦ Ask the children to think about journeys during the day. They need to think of (but keep secret from the others) a journey at school today and a landmark in it they thought important. (Remember *Where am I?* (Activity 47).)

✦ The children must draw a map showing the journey and mark their landmark with a '?'.

✦ Let children play partner or small group games. Can partners identify each other's landmark? Encourage questions about the maps.

✦ Finish by using your projector or scanner and IWB for children to challenge the whole class to name their landmark '?'.

116. **Who's that on the carpet?** KS1, KS2

✦   Surprise the children by joining them on the carpet at story time.

✦   Take the opportunity to casually demonstrate good listening skills, showing concentration on and obvious enjoyment of the story your TA is reading.

✦   Your own voice, face and eye contact are excellent for the children's listening skills, but varying the story time experience will help the children's concentration and ability to listen.

✦   Consider other alternatives to make story time different: invite a professional Storyteller; play an audio tape (for example, Martin Jarvis's excellent readings of *Just William*); or pre-record your own reading.

117. **Test the teacher** KS1, KS2

✦ Make this exercise fun by placing the emphasis on your ability to teach as opposed to the children's ability to learn.

✦ Tell the children that you want to find out what they think of your teaching skills.

✦ Ask them to think about their answer to this question:
 ✧ What have you learned from me today?

✦ Suggest the children write down three things.

✦ Let them compare results with a partner. Were any results the same?

✦ Make a display on the whiteboard of some of the answers. Ask:
 ✧ Which learning is most common?
 ✧ Which should I be most pleased with? (Perhaps a lesson objective.)
 ✧ Where should I try to improve? (Perhaps there is no reference to your numeracy teaching.)

118. **Awards ceremony** KS1, KS2

✦ Tell the children you have been making notes all day: now it is time for your decision(s)!

✦ Hold up envelopes containing your competition results.

✦ Open them and announce the winners of your awards(s), for example:
  ✧ Pupil of the day
  ✧ Table of hardest workers
  ✧ Most positive person

✦ The winners could receive team points. Alternatively, stickers would let Mum, Dad or Carer know just how pleased you are.

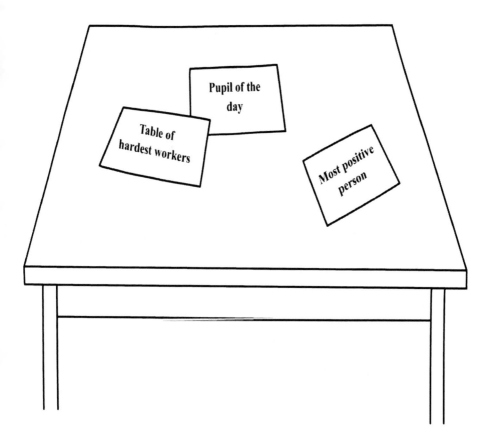

119. See you again!

✦ Remind yourself of *Hotel guests* (Activity 2). For younger children, what about donning your piece of doorman uniform from *Hotel guests?*

✦ Avoid forgetting to say goodbye to anyone by using one of your organized but fun ways of lining up from Chapter 3. For example, *Filing children* (Activity 33).

✦ Point out that for alphabetical order the children can not just rely on memory as absences will affect who is next to whom in line.

✦ As you lead or see children out, make sure you speak to everyone as you give out letters and say goodbye.

✦ A good doorman makes every guest feel happy at the thought of returning, so be particularly alert for children who have had little attention from you today. Have a special word as they go.

120. Who am I? KS2

✦ Return to this afternoon's *Clever clues* (Activity 62).

✦ Give the children time to re-read their clues and remind themselves who they are!

✦ Play a game of Who am I? in which children win a point for every clue they have to read out.

✦ Let the first volunteer read their first clue. The class then has one guess at identifying the character.

✦ If the answer is wrong, the volunteer wins one point, and reads the next clue. The class then has another guess.

✦ The winner is the person who wins most points by having to read most clues, so concealing the identity of their character longest.

✦ Does anyone beat the class by having to read out all 10 clues?

121. **Changing teachers**

✦ Play a quick game similar to *Who am I?* (previous activity) in which you are the only challenger.

✦ Tell the children that you have swapped places with another teacher in the school!

✦ Adapt the number or level of difficulty of the clues to suit your class. Older children may need three fairly obscure clues to the identity of the other teacher; younger children five simple ones.

✦ Suggest the children work in small groups, with each group having only one answer that they write on an individual whiteboard.

✦ When you say 'Show-me!' each group holds up their board. Have you fooled them all?

122. **Time for tea!**

✦   Tell the children how hungry you are!

✦   Show the children your plate of food from *Picture the food* (Activity 63).

✦   Use an alliterative phrase to name the food you plan to eat.
    For example:
    ✧ chunky chocolate
    ✧ buttered bread

✦   Let the children work independently or with a partner as they think of an alliterative phrase for the foods on their plates.

✦   Listen to the mouth-watering ideas. If children become stuck for words, you could provide the adjective (sizzling), the children only the noun (sausages).

✦   Repeat the exercise, asking the children to be ready to repeat their phrase or say a new one to create a live performance of a class food poem.

123. **Fly the flag** KS2

✦   Make this activity a follow-up to *Let's go to ...* (Activity 59).

✦   Ask the children to collect together their set of flags.

✦   Without looking at the names, do they know which flag is for which country?

✦   Suggest they use a partner to test each other.

✦   Finish with a class game:
  ✧ when you say a country, the children hold up and wave the appropriate flag;
  ✧ when you wave a flag, the children shout out the country.

124. The 'hello' game KS2

◆ Extend the flag game (previous activity) to speaking the languages.

◆ Write Hello on the whiteboard.

◆ Write and say these words:
  ◇ Bonjour
  ◇ Hola
  ◇ Guten Tag
  ◇ Ciao

◆ Ask What do they all mean? (Hello.)

◆ Give partners a few minutes to try matching a greeting to a language. See who has got them right. (French, Spanish, German, Italian.)

◆ Go over the answers a few times, before you play a game of Wave the flag: You say the greeting; the children wave the correct flag.

◆ Are the children ready to say Hello? This time you wave your flag; the children all call the appropriate greeting.

125. **Time to say goodbye** KS2

✦ Suggest the children are ready to extend their language skills.

✦ Write Goodbye on the whiteboard.

✦ Without saying which is which, write the French, Spanish, German and Italian equivalents on the whiteboard. (Au revoir; Adios; Auf Wiedersehen!; Arrivederci.)

✦ Are the children able to match any of them?

✦ Agree which is which. Go over them a few times and use partner work, before you play the new game:
  ✧ The children make a group of four, each child representing a country and holding the appropriate flag.
  ✧ As you say goodbye in their language, that 'country' sits down.
  ✧ The group with the correct 'country' left standing at the end scores full points.

126. Let's sing KS1, KS2

✦   Make sure the children have already written their songs in *Marching songs* (Activity 68).

✦   Let the children refresh their memories, perhaps trying the lyrics out on a partner.
  - ✧   Do they want to make any changes?
  - ✧   Does their partner have any suggestions?

✦   Now is the difficult part! What will the tune be? Let partners rehearse with one or both of their songs. Are they happy to present to another pair?

✦   Does anyone want to let the whole class listen?

✦   If necessary, spend a few end-of-day sessions on this, recording final presentations.

✦   Select from the recorded 'songbook' every time the class feels like marching to a new tune.

127. Storyland characters

✦ Write on the whiteboard pairs of fictional characters.

✦ Make sure they are characters known to the children. For example, Hansel and Gretel; Red Riding Hood and the Wolf; Cinderella and her Stepmother; Goldilocks and Father Bear.

✦ Ask the children, in pairs, to take the roles of two of the characters.

✦ Take a wander through Storyland. As you move around the class, listen to the pairs' improvised conversations.

✦ Let the children keep their conversations short and change to new characters when ready. Sometimes stop the class so you can all eavesdrop on a chattering pair. Is it obvious who the characters are?

✦ Put the children into groups of about four to extend the drama. Which part of which story will they mime or act? Can watchers recognize the characters and what is happening?

128. **Music time** KS1, KS2

✦ Read a poem or extract to the children. Choose one with varying actions and sounds (for example, Robert Browning's *The Pied Piper of Hamelin*).

✦ Suggest the reading would be improved by accompanying music, but the words must still be heard.

✦ Put the children into groups of four to six, with a box of musical instruments for each group.

✦ Let groups decide who will play what and when. They may want to share the task of saying the words of the poem or leave it to one of the group.

✦ After rehearsal, let each group perform in turn.

✦ Have a grand finale. You and the children who are not playing an instrument recite the poem while the rest of the class plays.

✦ Does the class vote it a hit?

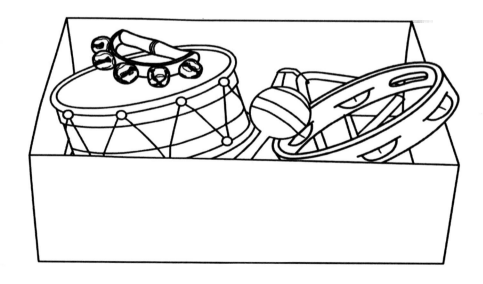

129. How was your day? KS1, KS2

✦ Tell the children about your day. What was the best part? What was the worst?

✦ In paired conversations let the children have similar discussions.

✦ Can partners suggest to each other a way to avoid some of the bad parts tomorrow?

✦ As a class, share some of the highlights. Discuss why they were good.

✦ Ask. How can we make sure that there are more good parts in the school day? Make a class resolution that will help everyone.

130. **Time to relax** KS1, KS2

✦ Adopt a relaxed position, close your eyes, and explain you are in the middle of a relaxing daydream!

✦ Describe where you are (on a quiet beach) and what you are doing (lying in a hammock). Explain that this mental picture is your key to relaxation.

✦ Suggest the children sit back in their chair (or even lie on the floor if there is room).

✦ Ask them to close their eyes, and let all the stresses of the day melt away. Use a quiet voice to offer useful tips for relaxing:
  ◇ Let yourself feel light.
  ◇ Release the tension from your body. Make your hands and feet flop.
  ◇ Let soothing thoughts drift into your mind, and put yourselves into your most relaxing situation.

✦ After a minute, compare how you all feel. Does anyone want to share their daydream with the class?

131. **I-spy with a difference** KS1, KS2

✦   For younger children, play a game of I-spy with the simple format of telling them the initial letter of what you are thinking of in the classroom.

✦   For older children, make the game different by telling them how many letters are in the word.

✦   Give the children a chance to play the game in pairs.

✦   Extend the game to include a focus on spelling, sounds, letters or meanings. For example, a clue could be:
I spy something starting with c, and the third letter is m. (Answer: computer.)

✦   Ask the children to play partner and small-group games of this I spy, with a difference! Is anyone brave enough to challenge the class?

132. It's storytime (part 1) KS2

+ Remind the children about your plans for a fun storytelling session. (See *That's a funny story!* Activity 71.)

+ Explain that you have realized that hometime is often rushed, so the storytelling session may need to be spread over the week. Today you will make the start as story teller, using cards to help you remember what you want to say next.

+ Have your story prepared, with cues written on cards; six to eight cue cards will be about right.

+ Tell your story, promising the children that their turn will come later in the week!

+ Follow this activity with *What's my cue?* (Activity 72).

133. It's storytime (part 2)

◆   Suggest partners refresh their memories and work out who
will tell which part of their story.(See *That's a funny story!*
Activity 71.)

◆   Emphasize important factors in your successful storytelling:
   ❖   interesting, audible voice
   ❖   variety in tone
   ❖   eye contact with audience
   ❖   appropriate facial expression and gesture.

◆   Let partners begin by storytelling to another pair of children
before progressing to group and whole class story telling.

Index

Page number

Active answers 29
Add the words.................60
After you 34
Afternoon blog 55
A is for 83
All at sea 76
All in a ring 86
Alliterative answers 46
At the bus stop.................36
Awards ceremony.................107
Balanced eaters 52
Book critics 11
Breakfast buns 25
Bulls Eye! 15
Catch this mood! 75
Changing teachers 110
Classroom code (part 1) 73
Classroom code (part 2).................73
Clever clues 56
Clocking off 102
Clues to the past 19
Cross the bridge.................42
Dear Ed 53
D for deportment 44
Discovery of the week 69
Eat well! 52
Ed says 87
Filing children 33
Find the solution! 72
Fishy folk 55
Fly the flag 112
Follow on 91
Follow that story 71
Football fit!.................44
Funny names 29
Guesstimate 90
Happy as we go!................. 47
Hear the signs 85
Hello, hello, hello 30
Help wanted! 16
Hit the target 13
Hotel satisfaction 101
Hotel guests 9

Page number

How does it work? 66
How was your day? 118
Humming bees 46
I never knew that! 69
In role 31
Instant growing.................43
Interactive story fun 100
In the news 14
In the post 20
I-spy with a difference 120
Is that my name?.................34
It's storytime (Part 1) 121
It's storytime (Part 2).................122
Ladder scramble 19
Landmarks 24
Let's go to 54
Let's sing 115
Look out! 48
Lost for words! 62
Making improvements.................80
Marching songs 61
Memorable mnemonics 22
Mini-workout.................37
Monday morning smiles 9
Morning Sudoku 18
Musical inspirations 57
Music time 117
Observation!.................47
On the catwalk 94
On TV! 12
Opposites 97
Parachute fun 77
Passports, please 17
Pass the question parcel 74
Picture the food 56
Picture the story 59
Pipedreams.................79
Pleased to meet you! 92
Pond challenge 84
Postboxes 17
Quizmaster 48
Recharge the brain battery.................89
School landmarks 104

Page number

See you again! 108
Shipwreck survivors 78
Shopping trolleys 21
Soothometer 82
Spellcheck 26
Spot the Chief 70
Square dancing 95
Still waiting for that bus! 63
Storyland characters 116
Strange sayings 14
Stress-buster 65
Switch off! Switch on! 93
Take five! 96
Talking food 28
Talking leisure 28
Target points 41
Target totals 99
Teacher in trouble! 21
Test the teacher 106
That's a funny story! 64
The big conversation 102
The 'hello' game 113
The magic talk box 68
Time for everything 51
Time for tea! 111

Time management 103
Time to relax 119
Time to say goodbye 114
Today's words are 26
Toss the rhyme 81
Tricky trolleys 22
Wakey! Wakey! 35
Walking dictionaries 38
Walking filing cabinets 40
Walk like ... mice 42
Weather watchers 24
We have a problem! 72
Well done! 87
What a rush! 10
What's my cue? 65
What will I say? 58
Where am I? 45
Whisper, whisper 49
Who am I? 109
Who's that on the carpet? 105
Word associations 91
X marks the spot 23

100+ Fun Ideas for …

… Practicing Modern Foreign Languages

137 tried and tested activities which can be used to develop oracy and literacy skills in any language.

Enjoyable, interactive activities that are guaranteed to get an enthusiastic response from all pupils.

Covers most of the oracy and literacy objectives in the KS2 Framework for languages.

… Art Activities

Easy to prepare and enjoyable activities that children will love.

The activites in this book introduce a wide range of art skills and media, and are compatible with the National Curriculum. Activities are suitable for use both in the classroom, at home or in children's clubs. Although primarily aimed at 7–11 year olds, most of the activities can be adapted for younger children.

100+ Fun Ideas for ...

... Science Investigation

This book contains exciting, fun classroom experiments to help teach scientific investigation.

The activities require a minimum of preparation and only the simplest of science equipment. Each activity provides opportunities for children to develop their skills of scientific enquiry.

The easy-to-use layout, closely matches the statutory and non-statutory guide-lines and schemes of work for Key Stages 1 and 2, will make this an invaluable book for all primary teachers.

... Playground Games

Make outdoor playtime fun and enjoyable with this wonderful collection of traditional and new games that will soon become playground favourites.

Aimed at KS1 and KS2 pupils, activities will suit individual pupils, groups or even the whole class.

Uses readily available equipment such as balls and skipping ropes.

... Wet Playtimes

Provides useful ways to keep KS1 and KS2 pupils occupied during wet playtimes.

Activities have an educational element, where games range from pen and paper games to word games, talking games and even group games.

Games can be easily adapted to suit all primary school children.

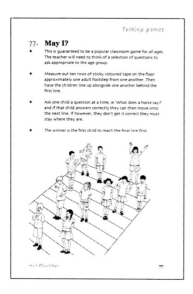